Teach English in Italy

Frank Adamo
TeachItaly.com

ISBN 978-1-84728-515-7

Contents

Introduction

If you would like to live and work overseas, there is no better opportunity than teaching English in Italy. You can enjoy many of the general advantages of teaching, such as personal satisfaction and long vacations, as well as the particular advantages of living in Italy: spectacular natural beauty, art and history, great food, local people who love foreigners, and a warm sunny climate. It's easy if you know how. I had to learn the hard way - through trial and error. But I've collected my years of valuable experience in the following pages for you to take advantage of. You can do it the easy way. Specific teacher training isn't usually necessary to teach English in Italy, but some practice will probably be needed before you become very good at it. This guide provides you with all the basic information so you will be well prepared.

It's important to understand why English teachers are wanted and needed in Italy.

English is already the international language of science, medicine, information technology and business, and English is fast becoming the international language in other fields as well. The reason is primarily economic. There are only about 60 million people who speak Italian, so the market for Italian language publications, for example, is very limited. Italian publishers cannot compete with English language publishers serving a global market with more than 600 million customers (one billion according to some estimates)! Most major employers in Italy see the writing on the wall, so when they advertise for new employees they specify: "Good knowledge of English required." In Italy there is even a fascination with the English language beyond simple utility because it's the language of Hollywood, popular music, and international politics. Many Italians want to learn English just for fun.

In addition, there is another important reason why Italians want to learn English even though they may not admit it openly. Italians have long suffered from a kind of inferiority complex. In the distant past Italy used to be one of the most important countries in the world, but in the last few centuries Italy has become a backwater of Europe. Especially since the end of World War II, Italians have been looking beyond their borders, drooling, at the "more fortunate" countries to the north and west. Today Italians admire almost everything foreign. Unlike the proud French, many Italians believe it's no historical accident that English is so popular. They believe English is a great language and deserves to be studied. In general, the only Italian students who still choose to study French as a second language rather than English do so because they think French is easier for Italians to learn - an important consideration for individuals with an inferiority complex.

Are you qualified? Regardless of whether or not you are a college graduate you probably agree that higher education isn't all it's cracked up to be, and many university degrees aren't worth the paper they are written on. Italians believe that more strongly than anyone because university education in Italy is even worse than in most other industrial countries. Many faculty positions are gained by personal or political recommendations, and in some cases are virtually inherited, so the quality of university faculty isn't very high. If you were born and raised in any English-speaking country (especially the U.S.A., Canada, Great Britain, or Australia), you will be considered better qualified to teach English than any Italian-born teacher - regardless of degrees. Diplomas and degrees are given weight when native English speakers are competing against each other for the same position, but otherwise no amount of language study or teacher education is considered equivalent to a lifetime of experience using English as your primary language in an English speaking country. Note that I'm not saying I believe it - I don't think you can pass judgment on a question like that - I'm just telling you what to expect from the Italian psyche.

Certificates offered by language-teaching schools such as the TEFL (Teaching English as a Foreign Language) and the Cambridge Certificate aren't necessary in many cases, and in fact many Italians have never even heard of them. You don't even need to be able to speak Italian in many cases, such as teaching advanced students who know enough English to communicate, but if you can speak Italian you broaden your possibilities since you can also teach beginning students and especially children. In any case your knowledge of Italian will improve by leaps and bounds once you are living in Italy, depending on your motivation, so don't worry about your Italian or delay your departure and invest a lot of money to learn Italian before coming to Italy. You may want to get your feet wet by taking a summer Italian course in Florence or other popular tourist destination, but that's expensive and unnecessary. The most important thing is your knowledge of, and experience with, the English language. The rest of this guide will discuss the details of teaching English in each segment of the market.

Teaching In Universities

"*Buon Giorno, Professore* Smith." If you're ambitious you can try your luck at getting a job in an Italian university, but it isn't easy. Teaching in a university offers a lot of prestige, but requires the highest qualifications. A teaching position at a famous university like Bologna could help you get a novel published, or make it easier to get future jobs at other schools or universities. Having taught at any university looks good on your résumé (or curriculum vitae, C.V.). The entry-level positions are called *lettore* or *ricercatore,* which mean lecturer (literally reader) or researcher, and correspond roughly to instructor or research assistant in the English-speaking world. Eventually you could be promoted to assistant professor, but full professorships traditionally go only to well-connected Italian citizens regardless of whether or not they are otherwise qualified. This is one of the reasons why university education is laughable. Tradition may eventually change thanks to the European Union (E.U), but if you want to become a full professor anytime in the very near future your best bet is to marry the rector's son or daughter.

As a *lettore* you teach regular classes, score exams, and possibly also assist professors in research and writing. Although most professors are Italian, almost all *lettori* are British, American, etc. Despite the high qualifications needed to become a *lettore* you have to be humble and maintain a low profile because you're at the lowest level of the university pyramid. For example, although Italian-born English professors may actually speak poor English, you should never correct the professors in public when they mispronounce words or make grammatical errors. Later, privately, mention that one of your "students" made an interesting error recently, and explain the correct form. Italians appreciate and respect decorum, and expect you to do so as well. You can find lists of Italian universities in directories in your local library, or through the Italian consulate in your country. The addresses of Italian universities may also be found on Italian search engines: www.virgilio.it www.altavista.it www.libero.it Some Italian universities have extensive web sites with the email addresses of faculty and administrative staff.

Officially, Italian law requires that teaching positions be advertised, and teachers hired according to the results of a public competition or *concorso*. If you are interested in teaching at a particular university, such as Bologna, you should subscribe to the city's major newspaper, e.g. *IL RESTO DEL CARLINO*. A big display ad will announce the *concorso* and specify how many positions are available, the deadlines for applying, etc. University web sites often have a page for job announcements. To find out what the minimum requirements are, or any other special conditions, you will have to read the full legal announcement or *bando* posted in certain official places like outside the rector's office. Theoretically, you could also call or write the university to ask when the next *concorso* is, but Italians don't like answering letters and you may not receive accurate information over the phone. There is usually no shortage of applicants, so unless you're a best-selling writer or department head at Harvard or Oxford you shouldn't expect Italian professors to be thrilled that you're interested in applying for a job. Humility is the word.

Once you've found a *concorso* in progress you should come to Italy to fill out an application form before the deadline. Theoretically you could do it through the mail instead of coming to Italy but since the announcement often comes out only 30 days before the deadline you shouldn't depend on the infamous Italian postal service. (UPS/FedEx/DHL all operate in Italy and are usually as fast and reliable as in the U.S.) You also need to get an official translation of your degree (a list of authorized translators may be found at the municipal courthouse or city hall). You should also have your résumé translated into Italian, and also attach publications lists and anything else that makes you look good. All such documents are called *titoli*, and you will receive a point-score depending on how many you have. There may be a delay of a month or longer between the application deadline and the next step so you can go back home and wait for a telegram notifying you that you've been selected for a written competitive exam and interview. If you have a doctorate in English and many publications to your credit you are a strong candidate with a realistic chance of being hired. But if you only have a bachelor's degree and no publications, keep in mind that the university's policy may be to send all applicants a telegram to come for an interview even though there is little chance that you will be hired. Even at smaller, obscure universities competition is stiff so don't invest a lot of money in traveling and get your hopes up unless you are highly qualified. Dressing well for an interview is more important in Italy than in English-speaking countries, because Italians place a high value on *bella figura* or what we might more disparagingly call appearances.

If you can invest some time in long-term planning, write and publish some articles in newspapers, magazines, or academic journals on subjects related to English literature, teaching English as a foreign language, etc. The credits may go a long way in finding a job. English instructors are usually selected by professors in the English department of the *Facoltà di lettere e filosofia,* even if you will eventually teach in other departments such as business *Facoltà di Economia e Commercio*, medicine *Facoltà di Medicina*, or engineering *Facoltà di ingegneria.* If you have special qualifications in one of these fields (e.g. experience in business or medical training) you might try writing to the relevant department to introduce yourself. It's possible, if not likely, that someone will take an interest in you and tell you when positions will be opening up. You might even strike up a correspondence with someone who will fax you a copy of the *bando* and application form. Since the employment contract for *lettori* must be renewed annually, there is supposed to be a competition every year. Even if all positions are already filled, you could be hired (and somebody else fired) because you have more *titoli*. Italy is the land of imagination, so almost anything is possible.

In general Italian university students aren't as highly motivated as we would like. That may be due to Italian culture, which is somewhat cynical, hedonistic and anti-intellectual, or it may be due to the bad experience Italians have in traditional (outdated) elementary schools. In any case, if you are tall and slender, blond and blue-eyed, you can expect to stimulate much more interest in your students because Italians are very visually oriented. As a university instructor you can also teach private lessons (to non-university students), and when you know Italian very well you can do translations for extra income in your spare time. Many books and journals published abroad are translated into Italian, and a few Italian books and articles make their way into English. Translating doesn't pay very well, apparently because people think it's easy. But take my word for it - translating is slow, difficult, and sometimes boring work. I charge approximately the same price per hour for translating as for private lessons (see below), and I would charge much more if I could. According to a recent survey the average price for English-Italian translations in Italy is eight euro-cents per word (higher in some places and for technical language). If you're working in the poorer south you might charge five cents per word. Don't sell your precious time cheap! In my opinion the ideal is to teach in Italy during the academic year where it's nice and warm, and then bring some translation work with you when you travel north during the summer where it's nice and cool.

Teaching in
State Schools

Teaching in elementary, middle, and high schools operated by the government doesn't pay very well but offers the widest geographical possibilities. You could even teach on a remote island if you prefer peace and quiet and fresh fish at low prices. The trend is to begin foreign language instruction earlier and earlier, with many schools now offering English in the third year of elementary school. A new law makes foreign language instruction mandatory in elementary schools. There is also a new project called the *LICEO EUROPEO* or European High School, which provides for the hiring of foreign teachers to teach certain subjects in addition to English. The Italian curriculum in the *LICEO CLASSICO* or Classical High School is old fashioned and overcrowded with subjects; students are drilled in such "important" matters as Latin and Greek and are otherwise discouraged from loving learning. That, combined with authoritarianism at home, makes Italian students difficult to teach. Italy is a mountainous country so most cities are on the coast and hence near beaches; on warm spring mornings the public buses are filled with students and their book-bags going to the beach rather than to school. But violence is relatively rare, compared to Anglo-American experience, even though Italian students are more passionate than students in English-speaking countries. A British teacher in Bologna told me that he was amazed at how extroverted Italian children are compared to his experience in Britain. If you like the security of working for the government you may be willing to put up with a lack of what Americans call school spirit. But unfortunately Italian teachers love the security of working for the government so there are many more teachers than there are jobs, and the process of getting yourself hired by a state school is somewhat difficult and a little complicated. I spent a year teaching English in a state high school under the old system, i.e. I was "recommended" by one of my private students who was the principal's best friend, so I was hired simply after an interview. That is more difficult nowadays.

Here's the official procedure. First you bring your academic records to an authorized translator for a certified translation, then bring the certified translation to register yourself in the local teachers' agency, the *proveditoriato*. Then you can take an exam of pedagogical knowledge called the *abilitazione*, which qualifies you as a teacher. Finally, you have to take a competitive exam or *concorso*, and your score puts you higher or lower on the list of available teachers, the *graduatoria*. As a native speaker of English you'll get a high score, no doubt. A school that needs to hire a teacher is supposed to choose from the best teachers available on the list. At least that's the way it's supposed to be. In reality, there is also the traditional matter of "recommendations," i.e. having an influential person put a good word in for you. Officially, such a practice is no longer recognized or tolerated, but I think it will be a long time before it disappears completely. Until recently you only needed a high school diploma to teach in elementary school, so there are a lot of under qualified teachers out there who nonetheless have tenure. Italian labor law makes it difficult to fire state teachers, so there is a lot of outrageous professional incompetence that continues uncorrected. New teachers now need a Bachelor's degree.

If you want to teach in a particular school you should visit the *preside* (principal or headmaster) in person to introduce yourself. I can't emphasize enough that Italians value personal contact and don't pay much attention to letters or phone calls. If necessary, hire an interpreter. When a position is open and no highly recommended candidates are waiting in line, the principal will be pleased to know you aren't just a name on a list. If you are able to communicate you may be able to cultivate friendships that could open the doors of Italian society to you. Most Italians love everything British or American (except the food), and some will be eager to learn or practice their English with you. (Communists are an exception; they tend to be anti-American and pro-Castro, but even they grudgingly recognize the importance of the English language.) If you are a woman beware that Italian men are notoriously aggressive and may misinterpret your friendliness as an expression of sexual availability. In general, feel free to go to restaurants or other public places with a man but be reluctant to accept an invitation to go to his home unless his wife - or mother - will be present. On the other hand if you are sexually available, be sure to agree on arrangements and preparations long before arriving at the point of no return. If you're a man note that Italian women expect men to be aggressive, so if you don't show great interest in a woman immediately she may feel offended. When you act very romantic she may laugh at you and call you a fool, but underneath the surface she'll be thinking that you're normal and healthy.

FLASH! Some public schools are now hiring foreigners for English conversation lessons, i.e. temporary assistant teachers who work under the regular English teacher (usually an Italian citizen), without any bureaucratic red tape. To apply you just go directly to the school's principal, introduce yourself and hand in your C.V. You may then be interviewed by the regular English teacher, and after an informal meeting of a committee you can be offered a contract for the coming school year! An Italian teacher told me that foreign conversation teachers have it rough because their grades don't count. Students don't feel much incentive to study or even behave themselves (i.e. be quiet) during conversation class. So you might try to arrange something with the regular teacher, e.g. making your grade worth 25% of the final grade in the regular English class.

In October 1998, the Schengen Treaty came into effect and established common immigration standards for the E.U., although each country retains different regulations. Working in Italy was easy in the past, but you now need a work contract and declaration of responsibility from an Italian employer to obtain a work visa from the Italian consulate in your country. Some teachers avoid the red tape by working under the table (illegally), usually teaching private lessons. However, without a proper visa you won't be able to rent an apartment - you'll have to live in a hotel or stay with friends or relatives. That makes you a *clandestino* and involves a legal risk for whoever is "hiding" you. Officially, "hiding" a *clandestino* is a crime. The legal route is complicated but safer. Unless you are a citizen of the E.U. you will have to go through some sneaky maneuvers to get a work permit, *permesso di soggiorno per motivo di lavoro*. Recently a lottery system began which rations work visas according to country of origin, with the U.S. classified as a low-priority country. That has led to an increasing number of teachers living on three-month renewable tourist visas to be able to rent an apartment and then working illegally. You have to show the immigration office that you have enough cash to support yourself for three months without working. A few American ex-pats carry around a copy of the 1948 "Most Favored Nation" treaty between Italy and the U.S., which guarantees the free exchange of professionals, artists and students. In theory,

Italy's current immigration policy is in violation of the 1948 treaty. Although the U.S. government is not likely to defend an illegal teacher in Italy, flashing a copy of the treaty in front of the financial police might discourage them from being impolite to you. Another trick is to get a work visa by getting yourself hired by a privately owned language school.

Teaching in
Private Schools

Every city in Italy has privately owned schools offering day and evening courses in foreign languages - especially English. Some large cities have more than 20 schools, and the larger schools have hundreds of students. English language teaching is a boom industry. New teachers must be hired every year because there is a large turnover in staff, for reasons explained below. Since privately owned schools are businesses, they require a profit to survive. The quest for profit often leads to dishonest practices such as making exaggerated claims to attract students, "With our miracle method you can be fluent in months instead of years!"

Classes are sometimes overcrowded with students at different levels, and teachers are often paid slave wages.

Many schools exploit young teachers for whom teaching English in Italy is a first job and a kind of working vacation. You are paid according to how many hours you teach, but there is no guarantee that you'll earn enough money to pay your rent. "It all depends on how many students we get this year," the schools say. Several teachers are hired in case some don't show up, quit, or have to be fired for incompetence, so there is rarely an abundance of work for each teacher. The few teachers who are willing to work long hours for low wages stay with the school, and the others go home disappointed or switch to private lessons. Schools typically pay you about 10 euros per hour to teach a class of up to 20 students, while the school is usually taking in about 5 euros per student or up to 100 euros per hour! Since you need at least 500 euros a month just to eat and pay your rent, you have to teach a minimum of 12 hours a week to survive the academic year, and many more hours if you include your travel expenses and summer vacation.

Some of the larger schools recruit and train teachers in Britain or the U.S. You pay them to learn Italian and how to use their particular method, which qualifies you to teach in one of their schools abroad. Lots of wonderful promises and no guarantees. Some schools are successful international conglomerates with branches in several countries. Their ideal customers are young and inexperienced and don't ask too many questions. I imagine that the people who run such operations were once victims themselves, and having learned how it works they've become the next generation of exploiters. A common trick is to hire new teachers every year to avoid paying for your summer vacation. They tell you that your first year of employment is a "trial period" for both you and the school. You'll only be paid for the academic year, or eight months, but if you and the school are satisfied with each other and renew your contract for another year, then you'll be paid 12 months for your second year of employment. The trick is, they never renew anybody's contract for a second year. The same schools place the same ads for Teachers Wanted in the international press every year. In some cases that may be due to the fact that some young teachers only want to work abroad for a year, so it's not the school's fault they have to keep hiring new staff. But the point is: beware. Don't invest a lot of money in an international move, buying new furniture or even a house, in the expectation that since you're a good teacher you'll have the job as long as you want it. Ask to speak to other teachers who have worked for the school for more than one year, and be sure that the same director who renewed their contracts will still be around when your contract comes up for renewal.

Even though private language schools are the least desirable places to work in, there is a big business in selling certificate courses on how to teach English as a foreign language. In my experience such course certificates are unnecessary; despite all the jobs I've applied for over the years, nobody has ever asked me for one or expressed concern because I don't have one. Be suspicious of web sites that sell such certificate courses as if they are the most important qualification a teacher needs. A tiny fraction of the hundreds of ads for Teachers Wanted I've seen over the years even mentioned such certificates as preferred, let alone required. One suspicious web site selling certificates had ads for private schools where the majority listed such certificates as required. When I attempted to contact one of the "schools" through the web site (there was no name or address for direct contact), I received no reply whatsoever. It's possible that at least some, if not most or all, of the ads were bogus.

An advantage of teaching in privately owned schools, if you aren't a citizen of the E.U., is to get a work permit. Once you're hired by a school you bring your job contract and declaration of responsibility to the Italian Consulate in your country. They will (hopefully) approve your application and stamp your passport with a work visa. When you arrive in Italy you must go to the foreigners department *ufficio stranieri* of the police station *questore* within eight days to register.

31

They will issue you a work permit, which also authorizes you to teach in state schools (after the necessary bureaucratic process described above), as well as teach private lessons. The ironic justice is that you exploit the privately owned schools as a means to become their competitors.

Private language schools can be found in the Italian Yellow Pages online: www.paginegialle.it (e.g. look under Napoli; Scuole di lingue) or the telephone directories of any city you're particularly interested in. One of the largest schools in Italy is the Darby School of Languages in Rome: darbyschool@tin.it If you're interested in working in a summer camp contact A.C.L.E. www.acle.org If you're interested in Malta one of the largest schools is InLingua www.inlinguamalta.com Brief descriptions of many small schools are in the excellent book *Teaching English Abroad* by Susan Griffith www.vacationwork.co.uk but keep in mind that private schools open, close and move often so printed information may be out of date. The VacationWork web site is useful for a lot of general information. My job list has the contact information for schools that have recently advertised openings for teachers in the international press. Even though many of the ads may be past the application deadline, the same schools sometimes repeat the same ads every year, so don't wait for new openings to be advertised. Apply whenever you're ready.

A recent search for teaching jobs on Monster.com (and Monster.it) yielded a lot of irrelevant want ads. The few that actually said they were looking for teachers seemed to be placement agencies charging a fee, rather than actual employers. I wouldn't take any placement agency seriously unless the fee is payable after they get me a job and I actually receive a paycheck. My favorite placement agency calls itself an "Organization" and gives the impression they're connected to Harvard University (they aren't). They set up "programs" for you to be a volunteer teacher in Third World countries, charging you about $3,000 to spend a month or so working for nothing.

Private Lessons

Most teachers who work in schools or universities also offer private lessons, and many independent teachers earn a comfortable living doing nothing else. For some students private tuition is the best way, if not the only way, to learn English. Each student has different needs, abilities, and interests, and private instruction guarantees each student individual attention. Although group instruction can be fun and stimulating sometimes, it requires that everybody be in the same mood at the same time - an ideal rarely encountered in real life. Most students who seek private tuition are actually graduates or dropouts of group instruction, or they need a private teacher to provide the personal attention lacking in their on-going school classes. From the teacher's point of view private lessons are much easier and less stressful than teaching a group. The trick is finding enough students who are able and willing to pay for your time.

As incredible as it may sound, many teachers make the mistake of coming to the wrong place at the wrong time and using the wrong approach in looking for students. You won't be one of them! To get started you have to choose the right place and do a lot of advertising at the right time of year. For example, certain cities are overcrowded with English teachers and should be avoided. The most difficult cities to find work, in terms of competition, are Rome, Florence, and Venice. They are the major tourist centers so they attract a lot of would-be teachers desperate for students because many local people have already learned English (including study abroad) in preparation for jobs in the tourist industry. Milan and Bologna are also overcrowded with teachers. In general, the smaller and more isolated the city, the easier it is to find students. On the other hand, poorer cities in the south like Palermo, Catania and Naples have fewer people who can afford private lessons, but there is still a substantial number of doctors and other professionals - and even a few wealthy aristocrats - who are in the market for private lessons. In addition, the cost of living for the teacher is lower in less desirable cities. You can sometimes earn the same income even though you are paying less rent. Once you are settled and earning a living in some little-known city off the beaten track, you can always enjoy yourself visiting the more glamorous centers on weekends.

Most students come by word-of-mouth, since Italians prefer to hire a teacher recommended by someone they know. Once you have become established and well known, you don't have to depend on advertising. But to get started you will have to invest in a lot of publicity. I've found that classified advertisements in major newspapers are well worth the expense. A small ad costs from 25 to 50 euros, but from a single ad you may earn thousands of euros over the course of several years from continuing references. Free ads in weekly "shoppers" aren't very fruitful, because the most desperate teachers, as well as Italian teachers (who aren't native speakers of English), advertise there and offer lessons for next to nothing. Lesson prices will be discussed below. To place an advertisement in a local newspaper you may need to provide your tax number, *codice fiscale*, which you get from the local tax office. In some cities they don't ask to see your work permit when they give you a tax number. When you advertise you may also receive a call from the tax police, *Guardia di finanzia*, checking up on you, but unless you have an office, classrooms or employees they probably won't bother you with an inspection. They usually only want to know if you have all your documents in order, and they'll take your word for it. They already have their hands full keeping up with the many Italian businesses that aren't legally registered and don't pay taxes.

Here is a sample ad and translation, to be placed in the section of the newspaper headed Lezioni Private:

"Madrelingua inglese, laureato U.S.A, ottime reference. Telefonare a Prof. Adams 329.815.0621, ore pranzo."

It means "Native speaker of English, American university graduate, excellent references. Call...at lunchtime." Other variations are "molta esperienza con bambini," (lots of experience with children), or "specializzato linguaggio comerciale," (business English a specialty), etc. Note that if you are female you should indicate it by writing "laureata" or "specializzata." The feminine "a" on the end of adjectives referring to yourself shows you are a woman and is important to get female students. Some parents, especially, won't hire a male teacher for their daughters, but I'm not sure if that's because they don't trust men or because they don't trust their daughters!

When potential students call you they basically want to know if you can help them, and your answer is obviously yes. Some students wait until the last minute to prepare for an exam, so you have to tell them that intensive lessons are the only hope - and even then there is no guarantee. Once you are established you should hesitate before accepting students who are failing, because despite your help they may fail anyway and then blame you, telling everyone they know: "What a bad teacher! I paid so much money and my son failed!" A real predicament is when one of your existing students asks you to help a friend or relative who's failing. In that case make it clear to all concerned that you will try the best you can but you can't perform miracles. Learning a foreign language isn't as simple as learning to boil pasta. If potential students aren't preparing for an exam you should ask them what their specific needs or interests are so you can plan a program. Some students won't admit why they want lessons, or they don't have any specific reasons. Studying for fun is, of course, the best motivation. The next big question is scheduling. Try to discourage students from scheduling only one lesson per week. Not only is it insufficient to make real progress, but in addition that lesson is sometimes cancelled so the schedule ends up only one lesson every two weeks. The minimum should be three lessons per week (plus three hours per week of homework), with five lessons per week being the ideal. Some lessons will inevitably be cancelled due to problems with health, work, etc. The freedom to cancel lessons is one of the primary attractions of private lessons. In a privately owned school, in contrast, if you can't make it to the lesson it goes on without you and you've paid for nothing. If the student insists on only two lessons per week, try to stipulate that if one lesson is cancelled it will be made up another day during the same week. One lesson a week is ridiculous.

The final question is price. The going rate is about 15 euros per hour for one student at the student's home or office. If the student lives far away you should ask for 20 euros. That price was high back in 1990, and students were willing to pay it because they thought the E.U. was about to revolutionize our lives. But now we've seen that very little has actually changed, so students no longer feel such an urgent need to learn English. The E.U. may indeed revolutionize our lives eventually, but it will be a very long and slow process - at least in Italy. So the bottom line is that even though the general cost of living has risen, students are now reluctant to pay 1990 prices. My advice is: don't sell yourself cheap. Don't offer lessons for less than the going rate unless there are strong economic incentives for doing so. For example, if students ask for a discount, tell them that if they pay in advance you'll reward their trust.   One month's lessons paid in advance: 10% discount, three months in advance: 15% discount, etc.

Note that some Italian teachers, especially math teachers or retired teachers, charge as much or more for students to come to the teacher's home for lessons. That's because math teachers are even harder to find than native-English teachers, and retired teachers don't need a lot of students. Don't overcharge for English lessons or you won't survive.

The students who are very interested will usually make an appointment to see you, while others will say they'll think about it and call you back. If you don't speak Italian, you'll obviously have to hire an answering service to handle your calls. You might try buying an Italian cell phone and tell your answering service to forward calls from potential students who can communicate in English. A disadvantage of cell phones is that students often call at the last minute to cancel or reschedule appointments. That's convenient for the student but very frustrating for the teacher, especially if two or three lessons are cancelled on the same day (usually Mondays) and then rescheduled for another day (Fridays!).

Another good way to advertise is to distribute fliers or handbills. It costs very little to have 1,000 fliers printed, and thousands of euros in income can result from a single flier placed in the right hands. You can distribute the fliers yourself in the city center or at high schools, universities, hospitals, etc. Or you can pay someone to distribute them for you, but you risk that the fliers will be dumped instead of distributed. In my experience it isn't very fruitful to post fliers on bulletin boards, but if you're lazy you could do that instead. The primary advantage of distributing fliers is that you can carefully target your audience. The most likely students are from 14 to 45 years old, middle class rather than poor people, and not highly conservative. Another advantage is that you have space to say more than in a classified ad. For example, you can state your prices. There are many theories of price, and I haven't done any controlled research, but I think that stating your price avoids unnecessary calls from unrealistic people who hope you give lessons for next to nothing. On the other hand, if you don't state your price there's the danger that some skeptical people won't bother to call you because they're sure your prices are excessive. In general, people like having a price list they can study at their leisure. Here is a sample flier with translation:

INGLESE !

- Lezioni private o in piccoli gruppi a domicilio
- Professore di madrelingua inglese, laureato Oxford
- Orario variabile/flessibile
- Nove dei miei studenti hanno vinto concorsi
- Prezzi modici più sconti

1 persona	2 persone	3 persone
2 ore/settimana		
100 euro/mese	150 euro/mese	200 euro/mese
3 ore alla settimana		
150 euro/mese	200 euro/mese	250 euro/mese
5 ore alla settimana		
250 euro/mese	350 euro/mese	450 euro/mese

Sconti per pagamento in anticipo:
1 mese in anticipo: 10% sconto
2 mesi in anticipo: 15% sconto
3 mesi in anticipo: 20% sconto
Per ulteriore informazioni telefonare a
Prof. (Prof.ssa) Your name & phone number.

ENGLISH !
- Private lessons or small groups at your home
- Professor is a native speaker of English
& graduate of Oxford
- Flexible/variable schedule
- Nine of my students have won job competitions
- Modest prices plus discounts

1 person	2 persons	3 persons
2 hours/week		
100 euros/mo.	150 euros/mo.	200 euros/mo.
3 hours/week		
150 euros/mo.	200 euros/mo.	250 euros/mo.
5 hours per week		
250 euros/mo.	350 euros/mo.	450 euros/mo.

Discounts for advance payment:
1 month paid in advance: 10% discount
2 months in advance: 15% discount
3 months in advance: 20% discount
For more information call
Professore… (if female: Professoressa…).

Note that Italians use a decimal where English-speaking people use a comma, and vice versa, except in scientific literature where the Anglo-American standard is used. The above prices are based on a rate of about 15 euros per hour for one person, 10 euros per hour per person for two persons, and 8 euros per hour per person for 3 persons. By "month" I mean a 4-

week period rather than a calendar month. Some greedy teachers charge up to 25 euros per hour per person, and crowd several persons together in the same lesson. Such practices are outrageous and I doubt that such teachers last long. If the student doesn't want to pay in advance, then you should require payment at each lesson. Otherwise the student may run up a bill and then refuse to pay, knowing that it wouldn't be worth the legal expense for you to take him to court. (In Italy a civil suit can take five years to reach judgment.) Always bring change with you, too. A common trick is that the student says he only has a 100-euro note, and when you don't have the change he says he'll pay you next time. But instead he calls you on the phone two days later to terminate lessons so you never get paid for the last lesson. Always bring change and don't be afraid to insist on immediate payment.

Another reason to encourage payment in advance is that often a student agrees on a schedule, say Monday - Wednesday - Friday at 7:00, so you have to refuse another student who wants lessons Monday and Thursday at

7:00, and another who wants Wednesday and Saturday at 7:00. But after two weeks the first student changes his mind and stops lessons so you're left with nothing. If the student has paid for a month's lessons in advance he's obliged to persevere, and once he's invested a month in studying it would be foolish to stop. Students usually have a peak of interest when they begin lessons but their interest declines when they soon discover that studying is hard work. The student's interest almost always diminishes eventually, but hopefully it doesn't happen until he's fairly fluent.

Ideally students should begin with intensive study, five lessons per week the first year to gain a basic knowledge of the language. The second year cut down to three lessons per week as their interest and need diminish, and during the third year cut down to two lessons per week to maintain their level. One of the hardest things about learning is simply sacrificing the time that could be spent in more pleasurable pursuits. So I always offer to go to the student's home or office for his convenience. In my experience no student who has to fight traffic to come to a lesson lasts long, while it's easier for the teacher who gets used to doing it all day long and gets paid for his trouble. For the same reason you should always schedule lessons for the student's convenience rather than your own. Having to fight rush hour traffic may not be the best time for you to schedule the lesson, but if that's the best time for the student, do it. Otherwise he stops lessons and you have the inconvenience of being unemployed.

When to advertise is extremely important. If you look at Italian newspapers you'll notice that experienced schools advertise in late September when academically oriented students are planning their year, and again in late January when students in trouble begin worrying about their final exams. I've found that advertising during other months isn't usually fruitful. There used to be the possibility for *rimandati* or failed students to retake exams in September, so there was some market for summer lessons, but the law changed. Now it's possible for students to be promoted on condition that they retake and pass certain exams in September, which to me sounds like the same system as before. In any case, in the summer Italy is very hot so summer lessons are pure torture. University students can still retake exams throughout the year, but the summer is too hot to study (or do anything) anyway so there is always some excuse to wait until the fall. Some students do begin lessons late, at the oddest times, but they are the exception rather than the rule. You should also try to maintain the same phone number year after year, because some people will save your ad or flier and call you a year later!

Private lessons offer you the greatest freedom. There is no job security, of course, but I've been at it since 1990 and I haven't starved yet. Occasionally Italy is subject to financial panics in which people suddenly become afraid to spend money. That usually happens when a government falls. They stop buying new clothes and eliminate all other unnecessary expenses, which has a domino effect throughout the whole economy. While unnerving for independent teachers (who are an unnecessary expense), such panics only last a month or two. Eventually people have to buy new shoes, and everything gets back to normal.

Another disadvantage of private lessons is that when students pay a teacher directly they want to control the course method, content, materials, and everything else. Usually that works out fine because it stimulates the student's internal motivation. But sometimes students are fickle and instead of accepting the teacher's advice they change methods and materials every month and make little progress - which is very frustrating for the student as well as the teacher. That problem seems more common with students who have experienced a lot of financial success, the "self-made man," so they have a high opinion of themselves and a low opinion of poor teachers. In such cases it's best to tell the student to keep his money and dedicate himself to self-study. In contrast, aristocratic families tend to be super-nice, they are models of courtesy and also ideal references.

I've read thousands of pages of modern educational research and found little evidence that any particular teaching methods are more effective than other teaching methods. The only factor that consistently correlates with scholastic achievement is internal motivation. Students who want to learn tend to learn more than students who are studying for external incentives. So students should be allowed as much freedom as possible in designing their English course, choosing textbooks, etc., with the teacher acting as consultant. Such freedom is only possible with private lessons.

Traditional Italian pedagogy holds that internal motivation is not only the best way but the only way to learn. If internal motivation is lacking, then threats of punishment are in order. But as a last resort external (positive) incentives are preferable to threats of punishment. I've found that external rewards are essential for Italian children, e.g. spending the last ten minutes of the lesson playing an English computer game, or watching English videos on occasion, if the student does the work.

You'll find that bookshops in Italy tend to sell grammar books and dictionaries published in Britain. That isn't a problem for

Americans because there are few differences in usage and spelling between Britain and the U.S. Some British teachers are spreading the myth that British usage and pronunciation are somehow superior to American usage, and that Americans tend to speak English incorrectly. If you hear such nonsense from Italian students you can point out that while British usage may be "correct" in Britain, and American usage may be "correct" in the U.S., there is no international linguistic authority that can decree which usage, if any, is "correct" in Italy. British scholars and the BBC admit that British usage is becoming more similar to American usage, rather than the other way around. Claiming that one country's usage is somehow superior to another's is to misunderstand the nature of language and communication.

Some Britons speak English worse, by their own standards, than any Americans. A British teacher I once met excused his use of "We was..." and "They was..." admitting that he only taught conversation rather than grammar. American teachers who use British books can point out the differences between British and American usage better than British teachers who have never studied American grammar. I like the Cambridge "Essential Grammar in Use" series because in the elementary book there are translations in Italian, and the advanced book mentions many "variations" in usage (which are actually American forms).

I should admit that I have a grudge against Oxford University Press because I bought the Oxford English Dictionary on CD-ROM a few years ago, and it wouldn't run on my old laptop with Windows 98, despite the clearly stated system requirements on the packaging. When I informed the publisher they sent me a "patch," which didn't do any good. My further emails to the publisher's technical department went unanswered. I subsequently discovered on Amazon.com that other people had the same problem, but rather than admit any mistake or issue refunds, the publisher's policy was, evidently, to stonewall its customers.

Thanks to the Internet it's now feasible to teach online. Commonly called "Distance

Learning," professionals such as doctors use online video conferencing for refresher courses, specialized training, etc. In theory, online lessons could also be used to teach English as a second language. In practical terms there are currently limits to the idea in Italy and other countries because connecting to the Internet is expensive. Telephone subscribers have to pay by the minute for all calls, even to a local Internet Service Provider access number, unlike in the U.S. where unlimited telephone use costs only a low monthly fee. Nonetheless, a one-hour Internet connection is still cheaper than paying a teacher to come to the student's home, and some students may even prefer it to personal contact. I'm currently designing a web site to test the market and will report the results in the near future. If there is sufficient interest, the teacher won't even have to leave home to teach "in" Italy. At the very least, it could prove to be an additional source of income for conventional teachers.

There are many opportunities for volunteering in Italy, especially in the poor south, which is satisfying in itself and also a good way to publicize yourself. In addition to national organizations such as animal abuse hotlines, many local churches welcome volunteers even if you aren't a religious person. All you have to do is walk around and introduce yourself. I have volunteered with poor children for many years, and although I can't say they learned much from me but I've certainly learned a lot from them!

The school year 2005-2006 was a banner year for English teachers in Italy. I'm not sure why, but I had more lessons than in any year since I first started teaching full-time in 1990. But I'm thinking about retiring so if you have some capital to invest, I can offer you a turn-key teaching job. I'm willing to hand my local students over to you for a referral fee of $5,000. You would have a guaranteed minimum of 12 hours/week of lessons, which is enough to live on. With a minimum of advertising you should be able to increase that to 15-20 hours/week or more. I'll meet you at the airport and introduce you to the students, help you find a place to live, and no matter where I go I'll be available for continuing advice via daily email. If you're seriously interested you should contact me at teachitaly2000@yahoo.com

So there, you now know how to come to Italy and go to work. Am I crazy for selling this information so cheap? Maybe, but as far as I'm concerned this is war, a war against ignorance. I love Italy and would like to help Italians escape from the Dark Ages. There is so much important information available in English - on modern educational research, health, the Internet, and even elementary logic - that is unavailable in Italian. There is some traditional wisdom in Italy that could contribute to modern Anglo-American culture, but most of the information available to Italian speakers is embarrassingly primitive. The Italian-language Internet is like a small town isolated in the mountains. The explosion of information available on Amazon.com alone is revolutionary and largely unknown in Italy. The only solution is to teach these people how to speak our language. Although English television programs and films (dubbed into Italian) penetrate every Italian home, they don't have the same effect as more personal contact with foreigners and our strange ideas. In my experience, when people meet me they are unlikely to admit they need to change, but after they have thought about it they do change and become agents of change for others.

Cultural
Considerations

Most people are familiar with Italy's history – ancient Rome, the Renascence, World War Two – but there isn't much information available in English on contemporary Italy. Some articles and TV programs in the English-speaking world about contemporary Italy contain information that is superficial and inaccurate. On one hand Italy isn't as bad as it seems, but nor is it paradise.

Italy's experiment with Fascist imperialism was a tragedy similar to Eastern Europe's failed experiment with communism. Italians are still suffering the consequences. Many Italians today still believe that when the Allies invaded Europe and helped set up the new democratic governments Italy became the world headquarters of the C.I.A. and a pawn of American interests. For all I know that may be true. What is troubling is that there is no concrete evidence available to the average person but many Italians believe it anyway and some even think it's a good thing!

Government services here (public schools, the postal service, national health care, etc.) are terrible (corrupt and inefficient) so many citizens don't respect the government and don't pay income taxes. Hence they want to believe that some great force is behind the scenes keeping the country from falling apart (a function gods used to perform). The resulting cynicism and hedonism are obstacles to any real progress. I believe that the warm climate doesn't encourage productivity, so air conditioning is a partial solution. Especially in the schools and universities, air conditioning may wake people up to the need to overhaul the outdated educational system. Better-educated citizens would be more responsible and more productive citizens. But even in the slightly cooler north higher productivity doesn't overcome mental inertia.

Although the popular image of Italy presents it as a very homogeneous country with no regional conflicts, for the past few years there has been a small movement in northern Italy to separate from the south. Some of those people are self-admitted racists and have engaged in violence. However, there is unlikely to be any civil war because the movement's leaders are getting too old to do anything. Contrary to the racist propaganda, the rate of serious crime in the south is actually lower than in the north, and is also lower than other European countries and much lower than the U.S.A. Although the official statistics may be unreliable as to minor crimes due to under-reporting, the statistics on relative homicide rates are certainly accurate since it's unlikely that many homicides go unreported. The south does have many problems, but you are much safer here than in New York City! I suspect that an important reason for the north-south conflict is economic. Some people want to make the south look dangerous in order to keep tourist money flowing into the north. Ironically, it may be the best thing for the south. While wealth has led to higher rates of divorce, substance abuse and suicide in the north, the extensive Greek, Roman and medieval antiquities in the south and Sicily remain unspoiled by busloads of tourists.

The famously close Italian family isn't all it's cracked up to be either. Before Fascism the Catholic Church had a strong influence on Italians but that has changed drastically. Italian mothers used to be saints sacrificing themselves for the benefit of their children (while fathers enjoyed themselves and did little or nothing to help), but nowadays – thanks to feminism – we have equality. That is, Italian mothers now enjoy themselves more and do as little as fathers! Or worse, in some cases the newfound economic independence of working mothers has created the phenomenon of the Tyrant Queen, mothers who are so oppressive that instead of encouraging autonomy their children are kept psychologically dependent up to age 30 or 40, afraid to move out or get married. Italy currently has the lowest birth rate in Europe. Hopefully this a temporary phase in Italian history. Italians tend to value fashion, and the latest fashion in other Western countries is to have more interest in children.

Terror Watch: while Prime Minister (PM) Silvio Berlusconi's government was in power and supporting the war in Iraq, the threat of terrorism was considered high in Italy. But the new government under PM Romano Prodi has announced an immediate withdrawal of Italian troops so the threat of terrorism should be much less serious. The latest trouble in Lebanon has resulted in an Italian offer of troops to help man a U.N. peacekeeping force, but the Italians are careful to emphasize that their role will not be to disarm Hizbollah. In general, security in Italy is not good. Cars are allowed to park outside MacDonald's restaurants, and at certain predictable times there are hundreds of people in there and sitting outside, so they are easy targets for terrorists who aren't particular about their victims. Always exercise caution wherever you go.

For further information on living and working in Italy the best resource is a monthly journal: The Informer. It offers practical advice on such things as taxes, insurance, driver's licenses, etc. The web site is: www.informer.it The

American Magazine has a lot of useful information about Italy: www.theamericanmag.com Some of the latest Italian news stories are available in English at www.insideitaly.com Jobs in Rome are posted on www.WantedInRome.com Some Italy jobs are posted at www.jobsineurope.com English games and cartoons on CDs are available in Italian bookstores or at www.mediaport.it You can start your own web site at www.aruba.it It's easier to get your own web site listed on Italian than on American search engines. For summer teaching/recreation jobs try: www.scotia-personnel-ltd.com For books on how to teach English as a second or foreign language visit: www.amazon.com and search under ESL, EFL, etc. Also check out ESL Magazine www.eslmag.com The British Council www.britishcouncil.org/italy has centers in Rome, Milan, Bologna and Naples. There is usually a library and other services available if you pay a reasonable annual membership fee.

Italy Job List

NOTE: Some of the openings are past the application deadline, but don't let that stop you from applying anyway. Some schools fail to find teachers when they want them, and may be desperate to hire you even after their academic term has begun. If you are especially interested in a certain city you should let the school know about your availability at other times. The same goes for schools advertising for teachers of subjects you can't teach. Let them know what you can teach; i.e. don't wait for the school to advertise. If a school states "EC citizenship required," don't assume it's a nationwide requirement; it is just that particular school's policy at the moment. Let me know if you find any duplicate listings, and also please let me know about your success. Good luck!

ROME English international day school following the English National Curriculum, requires qualified teachers with at least two years relevant experience for the following posts: ENGLISH WITH DRAMA (English to GCSE, AS and A Level) HISTORY To GCSE, AS and A Level KS2 TEACHER MATHEMATICS TO KS4 WITH KS3 SCIENCE and I.T. Applications by email with letter and C.V. Please include names, addresses and telephone numbers of two referees. The Headteacher, The New School, email: info@newschoolrome.com Tel. 0039 06 329 42 69 Fax. 0039 06 329 75 46. Candidates selected for interview will be contacted by email and phone. Interviews will take place

ROME PRIMARY TEACHERS (5 to 12 year olds) Seek passionate and innovative teachers (preferably PYP-trained) to start late August. Minimum 2 years full-time teaching experience. Please email CV with three referees to info@westminsterinternationalschool.org or telephone (39) 347 3662663. Website http://www.westminsterinternationalschool.org/

ROME Istituto Marymount, Via Nomentana 355, 00162 Rome Tel. 6623360(0070) – Italy invites applications for the position of Elementary School Teacher of English in a bilingual program for the school year: headofschool@marymountrome.org Marymount International School Rome is a Roman Catholic, private English speaking school, under the auspices of the Sisters of the Religious of the Sacred Heart of Mary. We are also recruiting for a RELIGION Teacher for secondary grades 10 and 11. Potential candidates must be practising Roman Catholics, hold a catechetical certificate from his or her Catholic diocese, qualified to teach religion, specifically morality, to high school students, and at least three to five years experience teaching high school religion in a Catholic school. All applicants should enjoy teaching teenagers, be enthusiastic, flexible, and appreciate the Roman and Italian culture and language. Interested applicants should send a complete C.V. to the school to the attention of Sister Anne Marie Hill. For more information about the school please visit the web site at www.marymount.it A knowledge of Italian is not necessary for the position.

ROME INTERNATIONAL SCHOOL Viale Romania, 32 Rome 00197 Italy Tel: 0039 06 8448 2650 How would you like to work in the Eternal City of Rome? Applications are invited from energetic, dedicated and experienced teachers for the following positions at this young and expanding British style school in the centre of Rome. Kindergarten/Reception teacher KS3 Science/Maths teacher. Grade 1 class teacher plus qualified school nurse/classroom assistant. Please see web site on Applications including a photo plus names and contact numbers of two referees, should be sent by e-mail, fax or post to the Principal, Patricia Martin-Smith: Fax: 0039 06 8448 2653 E-mail: head.teacher@romeinternationalschool.it web site: www.romeinternationalschool.it

ROME ST GEORGE'S BRITISH INTERNATIONAL SCHOOL

68

www.stgeorge.school.it St George's is an HMC school with a worldwide reputation. It follows the English National Curriculum to GCSE, and then the IB in the sixth form. It seeks teachers of the following subjects in the Senior School (KS3 TO IB): Biology Chemistry Drama ICT PE teacher with co-education experience to teach 60% in KS2 and 30% in KS3, 4 and VI form. The successful candidate will have responsibility for all PE taught in KS4 and all sports fixtures and clubs in the La Storta Junior School (age 5-11). Possibility of coaching a senior team/club if desired Senior School (KS3 to IB); Drama Latin Italian In each case, a subsidiary subject/language would be useful The core criterion is enthusiasm for your subject. Applications or enquiries should be sent by E-mail (secretary@stgeorge.school.it) or fax (+390630892490) to the Principal. Interviews will take place in London.

MARCHE Civitanova URGENT!!! We are looking for a professional and enthusiastic EFL teacher. British nationality and driving license are required.

BA and TEFL certificate. Full time contract. For further details please contact the school. ETON SCHOOL OF LANGUAGES - LINGUA PIU' Group situated in Civitanova Marche, on the east coast of Italy. The Marche region is renowned for its shoe industries, but it is also becoming a centre for tourism. The English language is increasingly important for the people working here and the surrounding areas. Our school provides courses in English, German, Spanish, French and Italian, but English is the language which is most required by the students. Courses are run by highly qualified, professional teachers. It is vital to us that all teachers are mother tongue, organised and aware of the students needs. The school prides itself on being able to adapt to the various requirements of language for specific purposes. We work in companies, with tourism, state schools and the Port Authorities. The general courses for the school include business classes, children's classes and language at all levels. The school works with various course books and organises regular activity classes incorporating the use of the multimedia laboratory. We are

70

pleased to offer the LCCI and Pitman Examinations because we believe it has contributed to the success of our school and that it enables the students to recognise their ability. The aim of the school is to provide a relaxed environment in which the students can learn and improve their chosen language. Address: viale Matteotti, 67 Civitanova Marche, Macerata 62012 – Italy Telephone: 0733/818081 Fax: 0733/778237 Contact person: Ms. MARZIA MONTECCHIARI

MARCHE Language School in Marche for sale. Rare opportunity to acquire thriving private language schools in the province of Macerata, on the Adriatic coast. Established 30 years, most reputable schools of their kind in the seaside area of Civitanova Marche (40,000 inhabitants) and Porto Recanati (12,000). Scope for expansion. Would suit enterprising teacher(s) or small business partnership. lorettamuzi@tiscali.it www.centrolinguistico.it

ABRUZZO Our school is in Lanciano THE TOWN. It is a small town in the county of Abruzzo. It has around 40, 000 inhabitants. The town is about an hour by train from Pescara, where the nearest airport is situated (Pescara-Stansted flights daily). It is half an hour's drive from the mountains and the National Park and fifteen minutes from the Adriatic sea. THE SCHOOL. Classes are offered to children, adults, teenagers, individuals and to the nearby Honda factory. Class sizes are typically between 4-8 . The school uses the English File materials for many of its students and also prepares students for Trinity Preliminary English Test, First Certificate Tests and Advanced Tests. The school has also produced its own materials. Lessons start at three in the afternoon and finish at nine at night, although there may be a couple of mornings as well depending on demand. Teachers do not work weekends. The school is small, clean and friendly and there is a great atmosphere. A TESOL qualification is desirable. Experience is not relevant. Accommodation is provided in a clean, well furnished and modern flat ten minutes walk from the school. All the bills (excepts for gas) are fully paid. Accommodation has to be shared with two other people but everybody has got its own single room. There is 24 hour free internet and computer access, use of a school car (although you pay for petrol) Teachers are paid a salary of 140 euros a week (more than enough to live on) and they are paid without fail every week (which is a rarity in Italy!) Teachers are also paid extra if they work more than 20 hours a week but are not penalised if there is less than 20 hours a week. If interested contact Lino at the following: linodp@tin.it

CASERTA Language school in Caserta a town ten miles away from Naples looking for two English mother tongue teachers with a TEFL certificate. Prof. G. Marino Director of Studies IL CLUB DI LINGUA INGLESE school of languages Via Ferrara, 26 81100 CASERTA Italy phone n°: 0823 326225 fax: 0823 357084 e-mail: clubing@tin.it

NAPLES The World's Leading Provider of English as a Second Language is seeking energetic Teachers for its centers in Naples, Italy. Candidates must be English mother tongue speakers with a University Degree. Valid EU working papers are essential. Knowledge of Italian Desirable. 1 year teaching experience. email CVs to lcferrara@wsinstitute.it Contact: Luigi Ferrara, Wall Street Institute

NAPLES Service Children's Education best of both worlds. Service Children's Education educates the children of British Service and Civilian personnel with the MOD in accordance with the National Curriculum. So, if you want to gain the experience of living and working abroad, and further your career in the UK education system at the same time, you can do so with us. Indeed, the experience we offer could give you an advantage when you return from abroad. Teacher planning, preparation and assessment time is funded and in place in most of our schools. ICT and Foundation Stage Setting provision, pupil/teacher ratios and teaching assistant support all tend to be better than in the UK. On top of this, our strong commitment to staff development means we offer high quality training and funding to release teachers and, since accommodation is rent-free for the first five years and heating and electricity are subsidised, the rewards are more than just professional. This post is permanent, subject to a satisfactory first year. Salary and hours will be in accordance with the SCE Pay and Conditions Document, which mirrors the DfES document, according to qualifications and experience. PRIMARY BRITISH FORCES SCHOOL, NAPLES ASSISTANT HEADTEACHER Salary Range L4 (£36,705) - L8 (£40,512) . A vacancy exists for a full time Assistant Headteacher to join the leadership team of this small, vibrant primary school which recently underwent a successful Ofsted inspection. An excellent and experienced class teacher is required to take a full role in the life of this thriving primary school. The successful candidate will work in partnership with other teachers to further develop the curriculum and will have the ability to inspire and motivate colleagues. In addition to being a key member of the leadership team, the post holder will also lead a dedicated team of teachers in either KS2 or Early Years (FS and KS1), taking responsibility for standards of teaching and learning in one of the phases. The successful applicant will have: A proven record of excellent practice and team leadership. A range of experience across the primary phase High expectations and a clear vision of educational excellence Good interpersonal and communication skills Commitment and energy to promote the continued development of the curriculum to drive standards forward. We can offer: Children who are happy, confident and want to learn The chance to join a team of hard working, committed staff A school with a positive, caring ethos Opportunities for continued professional development ÷ Non contact time to carry out this important role A well resourced working environment BFS Naples is located in Lago Patria, near the coast to the north of Naples. It is ideally situated to explore the Amalfi coastline, Pompeii, Rome, Naples and the surrounding countryside. For more detailed information please contact the Headteacher at email: sce.naples@sceschools.com Posts in Naples are permanent with SCE and will require at least two years at the British School, after this and if it is in the management interest, there is a possibility to extend for a further period. Thereafter SCE will guarantee an appointment in another of its schools. Interviews will take place at the School. This post requires an Enhanced Disclosure from the CRB. All applicants must be experienced with a UK recognised teaching qualification. If you have been resident outside of the UK for any time in the last five years you must e-mail for advice. This post attracts an excellent financial package including an Overseas Teachers' Recruitment Allowance currently of £3,916. In addition a tax-free Cost of Living Allowance (COLA) is payable. This is variable and related to family size. A tax-free transfer grant of £1,373 (single/married unaccompanied) and £2,258 (married) is also payable. Superannuation is in accordance with the TSS. Further details of this very attractive recruitment package will be included in the information pack. For an application pack for the above post, please contact: Personnel Section (Recruitment), HQ SCE, Building 5, Wegberg Military Complex, BFPO 40. Fax 00 49 2161 908 2625, e-mail recruitment.hq@sceschools.com quoting the Ex Reference number. Completed applications are to be sent to, Personnel Section (Recruitment), HQ SCE, Building 5, Wegberg Military Complex, BFPO 40. Fax 0049.2161.908.2625, e-mail recruitment.hq@sceschools.com To ensure that your application arrives before the closing date you are strongly advised to send a copy by fax or e-mail in the first instance, however a hard copy must follow by post. You can access our web site www.sceschools.com for further information. Service Children's Education is committed to safeguarding and promoting the welfare of children and young people and expects all staff to share in this commitment. The MOD is an Equal Opportunities employer and seeks to reflect the diverse community it serves. Applications are welcome from anyone who meets the stated requirements. SERVICE CHILDREN'S EDUCATION IS AN AGENCY OF THE MINISTRY OF DEFENCE

CALABRIA private language school in Vibo Valentia, is looking for a new permanent member of staff to start this October. The school year runs from October to June inclusive. The candidate should have a degree, a TEFL qualification and/or some experience of teaching English as a foreign language and be a mother-tongue speaker of English. Some knowledge of Italian would be an advantage. You would only be required to teach for 20 hours in the afternoon from Monday to Thursday, which leaves plenty of time to travel and/or to supplement your income with other teaching (provided this does not conflict with the interests of the school). Calabria is the most southern region of Italy before Sicily. Vibo Valentia is a provincial capital (population: approx. 34.000) situated on a hill above the sea. The nearest beach is 10 minutes away. If you are interested in the post offered and/or would like further information, please email sallymoore@libero.it

SICILY Language School in Sicily is looking for qualified mothertongue English teachers. Send CV,fax/tel   0932456613 english int.school@virgilio.it   Contact: English

International School Tel: 0932 456613 Email: english_int.school@virgilio.it

RAGUSA (Sicily) European House You will be teaching classes and individual lessons to all ages and levels from 4 year olds who cannot read or write to pensioners who have just started learning English to people who have already done the Cambridge proficiency exam! Most of our students sit an exam in June (either Trinity or Cambridge) and so our courses are geared towards these goals. Most teaching hours will be in the afternoon, usually from 4 to 8pm but some morning teaching is probable and you will have to finish at 9.40pm twice a week. Saturdays and of course Sundays are always free. Initially you will be teaching 18 hours per week but you must be willing to teach up to 25 hours per week. You will be the fourth member of the teaching team. Our timetable is organised in such a way as to guarantee breaks between classes (No 5-hour non-stop stints!) The cost of accommodation is not included in the contract but we have a 1-bedroom modern apartment in the city centre (on the main shopping street) available to rent but if it is not to your liking we will provide assistance in finding other accommodation. The cost of living here is low when compared to the rest of Italy and even more so when compared to northern Europe. Typical rents are from €100-€130 per month for a single room in a shared house while 1-bedroom apartments generally are around €200 per month. The basic salary of €745 is more than enough for a comfortable lifestyle. Please send CV with details of qualifications and experience, date of birth, nationality etc... with a recent photo. A full CV with at least one referee and a photo are necessary and applications which do not include them will not be considered. Piazza Igea 11 Ragusa, 97100 – Italy Fax +39 0932 228636 Paul McPhillips, Recruitment

SARDINIA Qualified experienced EFL teacher required Private language school (authorized by the Ministry of Education) located in a coastal town on the island of Sardinia requires a reliable, creative, enthusiastic EFL teacher to work with

children. info@westminsterinternationalschool.org
Telephone (39) 347 3662663. 6717691(0070)

TUSCANY Nursery teacher (3-5 year olds) single with British Passport start immediately small international school in Tuscany Italy. Curriculum IB Primary Years Programme. Early Years Teacher/IBPYP Co-Ordinator with Experience in IB-PYP not necessary - training will be given. Prepared to stay at least 2 years. We will train suitable applicant. Please send CV with three referees   to info@westminsterinternationalschool.org
Telephone (39) 347 3662663. 6717691(0070)

FLORENCE The Int'l School of Florence is seeking a qualified, experienced GRADE 5 teacher for September 1. Knowledge of PYP preferable. Only EU citizens. CV and at least two letters of reference from most recent employers to Head of School, Laura Mongiat at Head@isf italy.org or fax to +39 0552008400. 6795405(0070

PISA Westminster International School applicants must hold British Passports HEAD TEACHER We are seeking an enthusiastic educator with proven ability in school management and professional leadership in an international setting who is able to build on the school's reputation for delivering excellence to start 3rd term this academic year NURSERY and PRIMARY TEACHER To take up the position in September for a minimum of two years. Telephone (39) 347 3662663 for further information or send your CV with three referees to Westminster@csinfo.it 6567056(0070)

GENOA The American International School in Genoa seeks a dynamic Art teacher for its newly vacant Kg-9 Art position. The success-ful candidate will have the opportunity to create and lead this new program. EU/UK passport holders preferred. Must be qualified and at least 4 years experience. Send cv, references and referees to Ms Garra at info@asige.it 6698167(0070) adolescents and adults. Experience with exam preparation courses for KET, PET and FCE is highly desirable. We offer a friendly supportive atmosphere with opportunities for growth and career enhancement. Our family-run school is a member of the Quality First Group and has been offering high-quality courses at affordable prices to individuals and companies for over 20 years. The American International School in Genoa, Via Quarto 13-C, 16148 Genova, Italy, director@aisge.it theinternationalschool1@virgilio.it Tel. +39-010-386528, Fax. +39-010-398700. 6637331(0070)

BOLOGNA Principal Due to rapid growth of this Early Childhood and Primary school, the Board of Directors is seeking a qualified and experienced school administrator. The successful applicant will be responsible for the day to day management of the school. Be the educational leader of the school. Have a responsibility for planning the future development of the school. Please email Sally Graham, Secretary info@isbologna.com for an information pack on the position and application process. Also requires suitably qualified, experienced and enthusiastic home-room teachers: one for 4/5 year-olds and the other for 6/7 year-olds. Please send letter of application and CV (including contact numbers for two recent referees) to Penny Henry on 0039 051 644 9954 after 2.30. Applicants should hold an EU passport. 6690691(0070) Tim Cunningham at above e-mail. 6623314(0070).

IMOLA inlingua is a small but busy school and is looking for teachers for contract from. Driving license essential. Accommodation available. via Fratelli Bandiera, 12 Imola, Bologna 40026 – Italy www.inlingua.it Fax 0039 0542 32260 Ms Phillipa Rose, Director

MODENA International School of Modena founded in 1998 as a company school by 'Tetra Pak' in collaboration with the International School of Milan. It caters for an international student population and is about to implement an ambitious development plan that will involve building a new campus followed by a rapid expansion in enrolment. We are seeking a Principal and a junior elementary teacher to join our small, happy school You will be able to encourage and lead a group of highly-motivated pupils to realise their full potential and will offer a subject specialism in one or more of the following areas: ICT, P.E., Art and Design, vacancy for a Maths Teacher for High and Middle School students between the ages of 11-16. In return we offer a commitment to your continuing professional development; small class size; assistance with relocation to Italy, including language tuition; company car and a competitive tax-free salary in the first 2 years for British citizens. For further information please contact school - email ismmodena@hotmail.com fax +39 0536 911189 ; phone +39 0536 832904 We are waiting to hear from you The Principal will be responsible for educational management and direction of the development and marketing plan, I.S. Milan is carrying out the search. Further information and application details are included on the web site www.ism-ac.it or may be obtained by writing to jobs@ism-ac.it

TORIN The International School of Turin We are a school of some 420 students with over thirty different nationalities from Nursery through to I.B. The school is applying for Candidate Status for PYP this year and MYP next year. Required - fully qualified colleagues as follows: High/Middle School Maths - the position of Head of Department may be available. Elementary/Primary Teachers - the position of PYP Co-ordinator may be available. Elementary/Primary ESL Teacher Early Childhood Teachers Interviews will take place in London during the first week in May. Please send/e-mail your full c.v. indicating three recent referees to the Headmaster, International School of Turin Vicolo Tiziano 10, 10024 Moncalieri Tel: 0039/011/645967/6407810 Fax: 0039/011/643298 e-mail: employment@acat-ist.it Web site: www.acat-ist.it

MILAN The St Louis School, is a private, fast growing, international school, catering for children from ages 2 to 14 offering a curriculum based on the British National Curriculum. It caters for over 500 students and is a member of ECIS, the European Council of International Schools.

www.stlouisschool.com We are seeking enthusiastic professionals with a minimum of two years' experience to fill the following posts: KS1 and KS2 class teachers Responsibility posts may be available for the correct candidates. KS3 teachers Throughout KS3 we adopt modern computer based teaching techniques. Children use a personal laptop in conjunction with wireless Internet in lessons and at home. KS3 Teacher for Science The successful candidate will be expected to lead and teach all KS3 science. KS3 Teacher for English A generous salary, flights and baggage allowance, with subsidised accommodation and an end of term gratuity is provided by the school. Interviews will take place in London later in March Candidates should send their letter of application to the Deputy Head, Mr G. Rafferty, with a curriculum vitae, and photograph including details of two referees (with telephone, fax and e-mail contacts) to: grafferty@stlouisschool.com

MILAN Play English a full immersion bilingual pre-school, is seeking qualified Early - Year Teachers and Nursery Nurses. Knowledge of the High/Scope approach and experience in working with bilingual children, an advantage. The successful candidates will benefit advantages. A two years contract and tax free salary (QTS only) Professional development and training opportunities Responsibility incentives Free Italian language classes Career advancement Accommodation available Please send full C.V., copies of qualification, full details of referees and a recent photograph to: Mrs E. Papadaki - Play English Via Confalonieri, 18 - 20052 Monza (Mi) Italy Tel: 0039 039 2312282 - Fax: 0039.039.2320591 - e.mail: info@bilingualschool.it

MILAN The Sir James Henderson British School, Via Pisani Dossi 16, Lambrate 20134 (MI) Italy Principal : T J Church MA www.sjhschool.com The Sir James Henderson School is seeking teaching staff for the new academic year and offers an exciting and professional challenge to experienced and well qualified teachers. The school has a well established academic reputation and is a member of CIS / ECIS/ and COBISEC. This is a well resourced and expanding 3 - 18 mixed school of 750 students providing the British National Curriculum at all Key Stages including Sixth Form AS/A2 courses. The school offers an attractive package including a generous salary, fringe benefits, accommodation subsidy and end of contract gratuity. Initial contracts are for one year to cover maternity and the school has a genuine commitment to professional development. Head of Science Department Upper School GCSE/AS/A2 Physics Special Needs Teacher for KS2 - KS3 Teacher of Mathematics KS3/GCSE/AS and A2 Classroom Teachers for KS1/KS2 Teacher of Music in the Junior School (KS1 and KS2) the ability to contribute to Music at KS3 would be particularly welcomed. A wide range of extra curricula activities and events take place throughout the year. Teacher of Business Studies to GCSE and A Level a well resourced and popular subject within the curriculum following EdExcel courses. Teacher of Special Needs to provide learning support and

90

assessment to children in the Junior and Upper School KS1 - KS3 working in a well resourced Learning Support Department. Interested applicants should send detailed curriculum vitae to the Principal via email or fax and include the names and telephone contact for two professional referees. Shortlisted candidates will be notified and interviews scheduled in London early in October. Sir James Henderson School : Tel 0039 02210941 Fax: 0039 / 0221094225 Email: trevor.church@sjhschool.com

MILAN The International School Of Milan is seeking a Principal to lead its small but ambitious Monza Section. ISM is Italy's largest international school with over 1200 students and is developing an exciting new curriculum model based on the International Baccalaureate programmes at all age levels. The Monza Section operates an Early Childhood Unit and Elementary School about 10 miles from Milan. The Principal will be responsible for both educational management and for direction of a growth-oriented development and marketing plan. We are also looking for experienced Early Childhood Teachers for our First School in Milan, and a Teacher of English and Drama for High School Further details can be found on the web site www.ism-ac.it. Applicants should send a full CV with photo and the names of three referees to jobs@ism-ac.it.

MILAN The Bilingual School of Monza has the following vacancies for September: Elementary school coordinator KS1/KS2 teachers Early Years teachers Experience in working with bilingual children, an advantage. The successful candidates will benefit from: A two years contract and tax free salary (QTS only) Professional development and training opportunities Responsibility incentives Free Italian language classes Career advancement Please send full C.V., copies of qualification and a recent photograph to: Mrs E. Papadaki - Play English Via Confalonieri, 18 - 20052 Monza (Mi) Italy Tel.: 0039.039.2312282 - Fax: 0039.039.2320591 - e.mail: info@bilingualschool.it

MILAN Part-time MUSIC Teacher urgently required for St. Louis School in Milan, Italy to teach Nursery to Year 1, must be mother tongue English speaker. Ability to teach piano and flute an advantage. This position may become full-time in Sept.. For further details please send CV with ref. to pogara@stlouisschool.com 6648750(0070)

MILAN E-mail: baps.school@libero.it Bilingual Nursery School in Milan, Italy has a vacancy for an English mother tongue NURSERY class teacher. If you are an excellent early years practitioner, enthusiastic, hardworking and have at least three years experience working with three year olds, contact our school. Please send c.v. and contact numbers/e-mail address of two referees to Deborah Chilver. E-mail as above. Tel. 0039/0266109121 - 335/6470402. 6621023(0070)

MILAN The International School of Milan ISM is Italy's largest English-medium school with over 1200 students and a curriculum based on the International Baccalaureate programmes for all age levels. We are currently seeking to fill the following vacancies: Junior Class Teacher A permanent appointment Primary PE Teacher Middle School Science Teacher Further details of these posts can be obtained from our web site www.ism-ac.it and applications should be made by sending a full CV with letter of presentation, photograph and the names of three referees to jobs@ism-ac.it. Interviews will be held as soon as possible in Milan or the UK.

MILAN St Louis School www.stlouisschool.com is a private, fast growing, international school, catering for children from ages 2 to 14 offering a curriculum based on the English National Curriculum. It caters for up to 500 students and is a member of ECIS, the European Council of International Schools. The vast majority of teachers are employed from the UK. For September, we are seeking enthusiastic professionals with a minimum of two years experience to fill the following posts: CLASS TEACHERS for KS1 CLASS TEACHERS for KS2 A generous salary, flights and baggage allowance, with subsidised accommodation and an end of term gratuity is pro-vided by the school. Interviews will take place in London. Candidates should send their letter of application with a curriculum vitae, and photograph including details of two referees (with telephone, fax and e-mail contacts) to: info@stlouisschool.com 6662341(0070)

MILAN St Louis School KEY STAGE 1 AND KEY STAGE 2 CLASS TEACHERS required Sept for this fast growing, friendly, International school. Highly motivated, enthusiastic dedicated individuals required with mini-mum 2 years experience. Highly competitive salary, with accommodation subsidy & baggage allowance. Positions of responsibility may be available. Apply with letter, CV, current photo-graph and fax numbers/e-mail of two referees at info@stlouisschool.com or fax: +39 02 56610885. 6569434(0070)

MILAN The Bilingual European School Opportunities exist for qualified, English mother-tongue teachers to work in a modern, dynamic school. Knowledge of : "First Steps", Socratic Questioning, Bloom's Taxonomy, Multiple Intelligences and the Italian language, is an advantage. An attractive remuneration package is offered to well qualified, experienced professionals. Applicants for September. Contact: Jan Couper, email your CV to jan_couper@hotmail.com or Cristina Brichetti 6566830(0070) crisbric@tiscali.it

MILAN Well established bilingual pre-school in Milan, Italy have a teaching vacancy for a native English qualified nursery school teacher. The school is seeking applications from enthusiastic, well-qualified, innovative and flexible teachers, with a minimum of two years' teaching experience. Please send c.v. and contact numbers of two referees to Deborah Chilver baps-school@baps-school.it or paloschi.luca@mula.it Tel.0039-3356470402. 6547774(0070)

MONZA (Milan) The Bilingual School of Monza is seeking a qualified and experienced KS1

Teacher. Experience in working with bilingual children, an advantage. The successful candidates will benefit from: A two years contract and tax free salary (QTS only). Professional development and training opportunities. Responsibility incentives. Free Italian language classes. Career advancement. Please send full C.V., copies of qualification and a recent photograph to: Mrs E. Papadaki - Play English Via Confalonieri, 18 - 20052 Monza. Tel.: 0039.039.231 2282 Fax: 0039.039. 2320591 - email: info@bilingualschool.it 6541664(0070)

MILAN Well established bilingual pre-school in Milan, Italy have a teaching vacancy for a native English qualified nursery school teacher. The school is seeking applications from enthusiastic, well-qualified, innovative and flexible teachers, with a minimum of two years' teaching experience. Please send c.v. and contact numbers of two referees to Deborah Chilver baps-school@baps-school.it or paloschi.luca@mula.it Tel.0039-3356470402.

COMO International School of Como Teacher of 5/6 year olds (Year 1/2) Teacher of 7/8 year olds (Year 3/4) Small classes Beautiful Italian lakeside location PYP professional development Tax-free salary EU national, graduate, qualified teachers should send full CV with names and email/phone numbers of 3 referees to tcunningham@iscomo.com asap www.iscomo.com

TRENTO A qualified and experienced EFL professional required at an EAQUALS school in Trento, North Italy (Dolomites). 22 – 24 contact hours per week. Applications by fax (preferred) to 0039 0461 981687. VIA POZZO 30 TRENTO, 38100 – Italy http://www.clm-bell.it Eugen Joa, Managing Director

PADOVA Villa Grimani International School, Italy are seeking to add PRIMARY teachers to their staff team for September. If you are a qualified primary teacher with at least 2 years experience and an interest in international education, we are interested to hear from you. Teaching of English as a second language. Please send letter of application, curriculum vitae and the names of two referees to info@villagrimani.it 6691764(0070)

PADUA The English International School of Padua invites applications from qualified SCIENCE, MATHS, HISTORY and ART Secondary School teachers to start September. Please write with C.V., including a re-cent photograph, a telephone number and an email address to: THE ENGLISH INTERNATIONAL SCHOOL OF PADUA Via Forcellini, 168, 35128 Padova Italy Alternatively, you can email your application to Mr Rossi at eisp@eisp01.com 6660734(0070)

ROSA (VENETO) The English International School of Rosa requires KS1 and KS2 teachers starting Sept.. The school is situated in the beautiful Veneto region of NE Italy. B.Ed./PGCE essential. Min. 2 yrs experience. Send letters of application and CV to: The English International School, via Segafredo 50, 36027 Rosa (VI), Italy.

Tel: 0039 0424 582191 Fax: 0039 0424 582385
email: info@eischool.it 6660548(0070)

VENICE Villa Grimani International School requires qualified English mother-tongue K-STAGE 2 teachers, and NURSERY, RECEPTION and K-STAGE 1 teachers as from September. B.ed/PGCE essential. Min. 2 years experience. Knowledge of Italian not important. The school is situated in the beautiful Veneto region, one hour from Venice, the sea, the lake and mountains. Please send letter of application and C.V. to: info@villagrimani.it or call +39 049 893 3833. 6638725(0070)

VENICE European School of Venice Bilingual International School Applications are invited for the following vacancies for September: We are looking for highly motivated and experienced KINDERGARDEN and PRIMARY Teachers (Y1, Y2-3, Y5). Letters, including a recent photo, a full C.V. and the names of at least two referees, should be sent to the Headmaster of the European School of Venice-Associazione Media

(...) Sport, Istituto Berna, 93 via Bissuola-30174 Mestre Venezia Italy or emailed to: europeanschoolofve@libero.it or pao.furlan@virgilio.it 6665843(0070)

TREVISO International School of Treviso Via S. Venier, 46 - 31100 Treviso (TV) – Italy Tel./Fax: 0039-0422-541615 e-mail: de_grauw@dacos.it We require Infant Class Teacher Junior Class Teacher You should have four years' teaching experience, be open to new experiences and committed to teamwork. Please reply with a C.V. and a letter of application including your teaching philosophy and the names, addresses and telephone numbers of two referees. Previous applicants need not reapply.

VERONA International School Requires Nursery, KS1 and KS2 teachers. The school is situated in the beautiful Veneto region of NE Italy. B.Ed./PGCE or equivalent essential. Min. 2yrs experience. Send letters of application and CV to: Instituto Aleardo Aleardi srl, Via Segantini, 20, 37138 Verona, Italy. Tel: 0039 45 578200. Fax:

0039 45 565600. E-mail: aleardi@aleardi.it Tel. 6560904(0070)

N.E. Italy International School in Veneto region of NE Italy re-quires Teachers for KS1 & 2 and KS3 Science with Geography and Information Technology. B.Ed/PGCE essential. Min. 2 yrs experience. Application and CV to: English International School - Rosa, Tel: +39 0424 582191; Fax: +39 0424 582385; sc.inglese@tiscalinet.it 6563960(0070)

TRIESTE United World College Of The Adriatic (Uwcad) is a residential school for 200 students aged 16-19, from more than 80 nationalities. All attend on scholarship. The school is situated close to the city of Trieste, and provides excellent opportunities for those interested in the Italian language and culture. All students prepare the IB Diploma, in which the school regularly obtains excellent results. Like the other United World Colleges, the school is strongly committed to the promotion of international understanding. Teachers are expected to lead extra curricular activities, participate in community service

102

programmes and assume pastoral responsibilities. Required for September: Teacher of Biology/Environmental Systems, possibly with Chemistry Teacher of Economics, with special interest in Current Affairs Possibility of a position in English Literature and Language IB experience is not required, but a willingness to contribute to a demanding and highly stimulating international educational community. Successful candidates will undertake to serve as Residence tutors if required. Brief letter of application and c.v. should be sent to: Headmaster United World College of the Adriatic Via Trieste 29 34013 Duino (TS) Italy Fax: +39-040-3739225 e-mail: mendler@uwcad.it www.uwcad.it or www.uwc.org

TRIESTE International School has openings for SPECIAL EDUCATION TEACHER Qualified teachers with degree in Education and 2 years experience can contact Director at metzger@istrieste.org or fax 0039 040 213122. Interviews planned in London. 6538745(0070)

Opportunities
in Albania

Albania has finally overcome its troubled (but fascinating) recent history and boasts exceptional opportunities for teachers and especially entrepreneurs who would like to open a school. I taught at a private school in the capital city of Tirana for a year recently, so I have personal experience. Most people aren't up-to-date on the situation in Albania and are afraid to go there, so a few people are making a lot of money. Since the very word "Albania" strikes terror in the hearts of the uninformed, some background information is in order.

The country is unique in Europe because it suffered occupation by the Turks for nearly 500 years, longer than any other country on the continent. Formerly a Christian people (Orthodox in the south and Catholic in the north), most Albanians became Muslims under the Turks and remain so today, though few are devout mosque-goers. Albanian Muslims are similar to Italian Catholics, which is to say they are slightly more religious than atheists. The Turks had a lot of influence on Albanian culture and even attempted to suppress Albanian language books.

After ousting the Ottomans in 1912 there was a brief period of independence, complicated by border disputes with neighboring Greece and Yugoslavia. Little Albania's need for allies led to a close relationship with Fascist Italy, culminating in the Italian invasion and occupation of the country in 1939. With the indirect help of the Soviet Union, Albanians finally liberated their country once and for all and became fierce nationalists and somewhat paranoid of foreign domination.

Under Soviet influence Albania embraced communism, considering Stalin one of the greatest heroes in history. The Russians did do a lot for Albania, training engineers and generals, founding Tirana's ballet school which is still open today and widely respected in Europe, and protecting the country from Greece – which considered itself still at war with Albania for several years after everyone else had gone home and accepted peace.

Even if all this history sounds irrelevant, keep reading. The new Soviet leader, Khrushchev, got too friendly with Yugoslavia's dictator (and Albania's enemy), Tito, and the Soviet invasion of Czechoslovakia worried the Albanians so they terminated relations with the Soviets. Desperate for an ally and still serious about communism, Albania turned to the People's Republic of China which welcomed the little European country and supplied financial aid as well as military security.

When the military coop in Greece toppled the communists there, Albanians became more worried than ever, since the powerful American C.I.A. was rumored to be behind the Greek generals (as well as behind Albanian anti-communist groups abroad). By the late 1960s Albania was engaging in a toned-down version of the Cultural Revolution, sending intellectuals and government officials into the countryside to work on farms, permanently closing all churches and mosques, outlawing international cultural exchange, etc. An Albanian told me that you could be arrested for listening to an Italian radio station.

Then China became friendly with the capitalist U.S.A., which went against the grain of Albania's doctrinaire communist dictator, Enver Hoxha, so relations with China waned. Again desperate for allies, Albania finally turned to Western Europe, which welcomed the little rebel, especially it's former foe, Italy, where there was a big communist party. Under the Fascists, Italy had actually done a lot for Albania, constructing roads, uncovering ancient Greek and Roman archeological sites, and even today most of the beautiful old buildings in the country were built by the Italians.

As in other communist countries, Albanians proved inadequately virtuous to achieve the ideal of a communist utopia. Government bureaucrats became inefficient, lazy and corrupt, there was intolerance of criticism, and vandalism or sabotage of "state property" appeared. As communism failed in the rest of Eastern Europe and Albania's dictator died, a professor of medicine at the University of Tirana, Sali Berisha, led students into the streets of the capital and overthrew the communist government in 1991. The newfound freedom was somewhat chaotic, with people building houses on formerly government land, opening little shops in public parks or on the edges of sidewalks, etc. After generations of strict Stalinist totalitarianism that controlled every aspect of life: education, employment, literature and art, freedom was something strange and many people didn't know how to handle it.

The leader of the new democracy had no experience in government and made mistakes. One grave error was allowing an investment company to defraud thousands of people in a pyramid scheme. Countless Albanians sold or mortgaged their homes to invest, in the hope of getting rich quick, and lost everything they had. The foreign press mistakenly reported that chain letters were the cause of the economic crisis. Being used to expect the government to protect citizens from any possible threat, many people blamed the democratic government leaders for the situation.

In 1997 anarchy broke out as bands of criminals looted banks, stores, schools and government offices, and the police refused to fire on the looters. Citizens stole guns from army arsenals and thousands of families fled to Italy in desperation, where they were temporarily housed in athletic stadiums. The foreign embassies evacuated their citizens while some confused Albanians fired on American helicopters. Despite decades of pervasive indoctrination into the communist ideology of social cooperation, Albanians turned on each other with remarkable fury, including drive-by shootings of innocent strangers walking down the street. The leading criminal in the capital staged a march of his troops down the main avenue every night, firing their weapons into the air to assert their power and challenge any competitors. An Englishman who married an Albanian and lived in Tirana during the period, told me that every evening people fired their machine guns into the air from their windows to warn their neighbors that they were equipped to defend themselves. Order was restored only after an ex-communist leader was released from prison and took over the government in what has been described as a rigged election.

One theory to explain that incredible period was that the first democratic leader had made enemies by replacing the ethnic Greek leader of the Orthodox Church with an ethnic Albanian. This worried the ethnic Greek minority in southern Albania, since Albanians were mistreated in Greece hence it might be time for revenge against Greeks. So Greece sent agents across the border to provoke the anarchy, in the hope that it would give the Greek army an excuse to invade the country and make the southern part of Albania become part of Greece.

Nobody knows if the theory is true, but the new Albanian government (ex-communists calling themselves the socialist party) gave two government ministries to ethnic Greeks, which is odd considering that ethnic Greeks make up only 2% of the population! A period of stability followed, characterized by gross corruption and the rise of Albania's reputation as the new world capital of organized crime. A few Albanians, who had nothing at the dawn of democracy 10 years earlier, suddenly became fabulously wealthy.

International pressure for honest elections helped the opposition Democrats win in 2005, and the hero of the battle against communism, Berisha, is the prime minister again. The ex-communists are burning mad, threatening civil disobedience, provoking fist-fights in parliament, etc., but stability has continued for the past year and the E.U. is monitoring the country for eventual membership.

In contrast to the aging population of Italy, Albania currently has the highest birthrate in Europe. The country is literally overflowing with children. Education is *the* boom industry. Tirana now has several private schools hiring English teachers (see below). As in other Eastern European countries, pay varies from low to moderate, but the cost of living is low.

My nice apartment (one bedroom) was fully furnished, air-conditioned, with terrace and telephone, on the fifth floor of an elevator building within walking distance of the main square in the center of the city, all for about $300/month plus utilities. I looked at several apartments near the center and prices were the same. A similar apartment in Italy would cost twice as much. It's possible to find humble housing for as little as $100/month.

Local food (poultry and dairy products, fruit and vegetables, etc.) cost about half as much as in Italy, while everything else is imported and about the same price as in Italy or slightly higher. An exception is clothing and other items imported from Turkey, which are very inexpensive, but the quality is also poor. There is a big community of Albanians in Istanbul and a lot of trade between Turkey and Albania. Turkey is one of the few countries that allows Albanians to visit without a visa. Most countries not only require a visa, but visas are extremely difficult for Albanians to obtain.

It's nice being able to eat a sandwich or hotdog for 50 cents! An ice cream cone costs 20 cents, as do the city buses. A film at the cinema costs $3.00 (I paid only a dollar in other Eastern European countries.) Prices are similarly low for bread and pastry or any other fresh food. The local beer is inexpensive and of good quality. Cigarettes are inexpensive, reportedly produced locally with counterfeit American packaging.

The prices at hotels and resorts are the same as in Italy, which is a mistake. Few tourists come to Albania, and those that do are looking for lower prices. Once they are overcharged they aren't likely to come back. We'll have to see how long the learning curve is on this for Albanian businesses. There are some nice beaches and a lot of natural areas (forested mountains) with abundant wildlife, but nothing that would justify West European prices for meals and lodging while the local staff are being paid local wages.

Gasoline is imported and hence the same high price as the rest of Europe. I've been told that the quality of the gas is substandard and bad for your engine. Since the roads are also terrible, you might want to leave your car home. For example, the main highway from the capital to Greece is what Americans would call a local road.

Other Albanian "highways" are similar. The streets in Tirana are being restored so they are in the process of becoming very good, but while so much construction is underway there is a lot of dust, which turns to mud when it rains.

There are frequent power outages and water shortages, but the situation is improving. Petty street crime is virtually non-existent in Tirana. In the heat of the summer children play outside and people sit in the parks well after dark. However, the extreme northeastern part of the country is reportedly dangerous for lone travelers. I visited Kukes without any problems, but there was no bus service to the infamous town of Tropoje.

There is also no bus service through the extreme northwestern part of the country to reach Montenegro, and the U.S. Embassy was warning Americans to exercise caution in the area, but the Albanian press denied that the northwest is still dangerous. At least one travel agency in Tirana organizes private bus tours to the beaches in Montenegro in the summer, and prices are low. The most famous beach resort is Budva, and there's a nudist beach at Ulcinj. One of my private students is Montenegrin, so she has told me a lot about it!

Quality Schools International has schools in Tirana and Kosova www.qsi.org The Lincoln School has two schools in Tirana www.lincoln.org.al A high school founded by Americans many years ago is the Harry Fultz Institute (now public) tel. 00355-04-228-746, which offers courses in English, computer programming, graphics and technical trades. The private school I taught at was so bad I won't recommend it. The Polytechnic University of Tirana axhuvani@yahoo.com has several schools. The Catholic University (Rome) has opened a medical school in Tirana www.unizkm.edu.al info@unizkm.edu.al It currently employs only Albanian faculty, but future expansion is planned. Another private university that recently opened (a nursing school) is Krystal University, Rruga Durres. They also have Albanian staff only at present, but that's likely to change, especially if you have training or experience relative to nursing.

Private students are difficult to find because few people can afford private lessons. I used the same advertising methods as in Italy and had one doctor, a journalist and a few would-be emigrants as students. The latter had to prepare for tests as part of their visa application process. Unemployment is still high so many Albanians aspire to work abroad. The students came to my apartment and were conscientious in doing homework. They were also reliable in payment and we met outside of lessons for social activities. I charged about U.S.$10/hour, which was high for them but enough for me considering the low cost of living.

You can place a free ad in the Albanian Yellow Pages at www.albanian.com English language newspapers are at www.albanianews.com and www.TiranaNews.com There are two or three international bookstores in Tirana, including one in Skenderbej Square in the center of the city. An Albanian language site www.balkanweb.com has an interesting Tension Meter, which offers current weather-style reports of tension in the Balkans.

Albania is usually calm, while tension in Kosova is occasionally moderate. The U.S. Embassy's site is www.usemb-tirana.rpo.at The U.S. Agency for International Development www.usaid.gov The British Council has a new multimedia library and English garden in Tirana at Rr.' Perlat Rexhepi' P. 197 "Ana". www.britishcouncil.org/albania UPS/FedEx/DHL all operate in Tirana if you need urgent international mail or packages, but USPS Global Express Mail (EMS) is cheaper and the Albanian Postal Service works a lot better than the Italian Post Office!

Your Own Private School

I tried to open a private school in Tirana following the British National Curriculum www.nc.uk.net (all grades and subjects), and almost succeeded. Much of the information is indirectly relevant to Italy because many of the parents I dealt with were Italians. Along with an Englishman and an Irish woman I spent the summer of 2005 organizing the curriculum, advertising for students, shopping for equipment, etc. We learned a lot but when we didn't find enough students the first year we burned out and didn't try again. You can learn from our mistakes.

You'll find that many Albanians can speak, or at least understand, Italian. After the fall of communism most television programming came from Italy, so many Albanian children grew up watching Italian cartoons and learned the language without any specific instruction. Now many Albanians work in Italy so their children attend Italian schools and only visit Albania during vacations. Although they may learn Albanian as a first language from their parents at home, after going to school in Italy for a few years Italian becomes their second language. It's funny seeing Albanian children in Tirana during the summer speaking Italian to each other!

Today there is a lot English language programming on Albanian TV, and even at the cinema films are shown in the original language (with subtitles in Albanian), so people get a lot of practice hearing English. The Albanian language is very difficult to learn, with archaic grammar of brain-cracking complexity and tongue-twisting pronunciation (too many consonants), so English and Italian are easy for Albanians to learn in comparison.

If you've got some capital to invest and really want to be the boss, Albania is probably the easiest place in Europe to open a school. You would have to go to Latin America to find a similar situation. We focused on the market of international families, but discovered that there aren't enough foreign children in Tirana to support a school. Evidently, most embassy staff leave their children at home when they come to Albania. We suspected that might change if a good school were available, but our website and phone numbers remained active and there was little interest the following year as well. You need to accommodate Albanian children, of which there is no shortage. That entails many complications, but one step at a time.

There are numerous private language schools in Tirana, mostly run by Albanian teachers who charge very little. In theory, some students would be willing to pay more for native-English teachers, but we calculated that you would need to have an unrealistic number of high-paying students to support even a one-teacher school. So a full-curriculum school for the children of well-heeled parents is a better strategy.

We chose the British National Curriculum because it's both comprehensive and flexible, and hence ideal for an international school with students from different countries and different needs. (Since every state in the U.S. has its own curriculum guidelines, it would be arbitrary to choose one.) The National Curriculum is also fairly modern, e.g. mandating that sex education be offered from seventh grade on. We registered online with the British Department for Education and Skills and received a DFES number www.dfes.gov.uk We found two high school students from Bulgaria so we also offered the International General Certificate of Secondary Education (IGCSE) administered by Cambridge International Education www.cie.org.uk

Albanian law requires that any organization, whether commercial or not, must be registered in the courts with the names and addresses of the officers, goals, etc. We had an Albanian attorney draw up the papers as a non-profit foundation. Schools must also be registered with the Ministry of Education, Rruga Kavaje, though if Albanian isn't the primary language of instruction then you are exempt from the requirements of the Albanian curriculum.

The most important thing to do is find an appropriate location, because the first thing parents want to know is: where is the school? I know one embassy parent who chose a school primarily because it was on his way to work in the morning. I pointed out that it was a pretty rough school so his son might be the victim of physical assaults (or worse) by the local students, but as far as the parent was concerned that didn't detract from the school's convenient location.

We initially chose a location outside the city center precisely because it was near our first two students. Their parents became our point of reference and foremost salespeople. The location also featured peace and quiet and clean air, being some distance from the downtown traffic. No potential students complained about the location, but it may have influenced their decision to go elsewhere unbeknownst to us. We rented a three-room apartment (plus kitchen) on the ground floor of a fairly new villa, with garden and enclosed parking area (playground), for only 250 euros/month plus utilities. That price even included furniture, though it was of no use to us and we asked that it be removed. The two floors above were also available for eventual expansion. We also requested a short-term lease in case the school had to close for lack of students or bureaucratic problems.

Finding an inexpensive location in the city center isn't difficult, but prices are higher. Since most parents either live or work in the center, it's convenient for them to visit the school and also offers exposure to passersby. We eventually rented another, smaller apartment near the embassy street to accommodate students there, for 350 euros/month, which was not only noisy and cramped but suffered electrical blackouts every morning during school hours!

We printed up a brochure calling ourselves the "American-British Cooperative School" (ABCs), and distributed it by hand to all the embassies, international aid organizations, etc. There was little interest. One high school student from Egypt asked if we would guarantee his grades to ensure he would be admitted to his country's universities on a scholarship. As he was saying this I wondered: is this a competitor recording the conversation to entrap me? I said no way.

When September arrived we had only eight students of varying ages, mostly Italians, and since Italians like crowds they said eight wasn't enough. We could have scraped by with only eight students, hoping that more would register later, but the parents were concerned about social learning, and I have to admit that children's friendships are extremely important. There is some research on children's friendships that shows a correlation between early social interaction *with peers* and later social skills. However, we shouldn't obsess over children's friendships to the point that we begin to depreciate individuality. The quality of children's relationships is just as important as the quantity. As you may have guessed, I'm still steaming over the Italians' decision not to register in our school!

At the last minute I had a new brochure printed in Albanian to recruit Albanian students, but it was too late since the Albanian schools had already opened. We closed our doors and did our best to cut our losses. I'm convinced that if we had marketed to the locals in the beginning we would have found enough internationals and

Albanians to succeed. An Albanian who read my brochure said I should have also found some famous person to endorse the school, as that would impress Albanian parents. If you're seriously interested in trying this, let me know!

My experience is that Albanian parents are very conservative, so they place a high value on teachers being well groomed and dressed up. That impresses them more than degrees from prestigious universities. Although modern Albanian dance is very sensuous and many young women in Tirana dress provocatively (tight miniskirts and transparent tops), many Albanian parents won't allow their children to watch kissing scenes on TV, quickly changing the channel. Albanian schools are even more primitive than Italian schools, so Albanians don't know much about modern educational research. Don't try to promote experimental methods in Albania!

One Albanian told me the first time he went to an international medical congress he was all dressed up and eager to meet the American speakers who were the world's foremost experts in his field. But he was shocked to see world-famous American doctors stand in front of the audience wearing short-sleeve shirts and jeans. The American value of looking at what you actually achieve rather than how you dress, is foreign to Albanians.

If you want more information about Albania you can read one of the many books by the Albanian-American scholar Peter Prifti, such as "Remote Albania: the Politics of Isolation." (Onufri, 1999, Tirana). www.albanian.com/onufri The country's greatest literary gift to the world is Ismail Kadare, who wrote many stories attacking the former communist government. A bizarre story is "The Palace of Dreams," about a totalitarian government's attempt to monitor the dream-life of its citizens.

Visit the U.S. State Department's site www.travel.state.gov for the latest travel warnings. You can send me specific questions at: teachitaly2000@yahoo.com. I look forward to hearing about your success. Good luck!

Made in the USA
Lexington, KY
07 May 2010